A STUDENT'S
LITTLE INSTRUCTION BOOK

A STUDENT'S
LITTLE INSTRUCTION BOOK

JASMINE BIRTLES

BOXTREE

First published in Great Britain in 1996 by
Boxtree Limited, Broadwall house, 21 Broadwall, London SE1 9PL.

Copyright © Jasmine Birtles

10 9 8 7 6 5 4 3 2

ISBN: 0 7522 2282 1

Cover design: Shoot That Tiger!
Page design: Nigel Davies

Printed and bound in the United Kingdom by Redwood Books, Trowbridge, Wiltshire.

A CIP catalogue entry for this book is available from the British Library.

FOREWORD

If beggars try not to make eye contact with you in the street, Oxfam sends you aid parcels and even rats turn up their noses at the sight of your kitchen - you must be a student.

Did you know that arts students don't stare out of the window in the mornings so that they'll have something to do in the afternoon, and that maths students are the only ones who can explain why a 2.2 = UB40? No? Well read this book and you will find out even more.

You'll get the lowdown on tutors, rooms, courses and your fellow students all for less than a round of drinks at the Students Union bar.

So read this and get wise and remember, there's only one sure way of reducing graduate unemployment - don't graduate.

Clubs to avoid at the Freshers' Fair:
any that are based on your subject,
any that are run by mathematicians
and any that offer you free food
or eternal salvation.

As a fresher it's easy to feel inferior,
but once you've got to know the second-
and third-year students you'll find their
inferiority complexes are actually
much better than yours.

Join the Political Apathy Society
if you can be bothered.

• • •

Don't imagine that you will gain
social credibility by joining
the Rolf Harris Appreciation Society.

How to spot a Fresher:
anyone seen on campus outside of bar hours.

• • •

Don't trust student societies
that have oxymoronic names,
such as 'Christian Lawyers'.

You know you're too good for your college if you can explain Einstein's theory… to Einstein.

• • •

You know you're at the wrong college if you try to join the Monster Raving Loony Society and it's full.

Why you should wear a college scarf:
to save you having to make a sign saying
'please beat me up, I'm a student'
when you go to your local pub
called The Builder's Fist.

Forget the starred first,
the most important thing to achieve at
university is notoriety.

• • •

It's easy to spot a medical student.
He's always the last person
you would trust with your body.

Rich students are just poor students
without parents.

• • •

If you'd rather watch telly than read a book,
think Shakespeare is overrated and
don't know where the lecture halls are
you're an English student.

Homework can kill you
if done properly.

• • •

There's only one difference between an
arts student and a waste paper basket –
a waste paper basket can hold more facts.

A student in a punt is
a complete and utter…

• • •

Arts students don't stare out of the window
in the morning so that they have
something to do in the afternoon.

15

There's not much to choose
between a student kitchen
and a rubbish dump…
except that rats won't go
into student kitchens.

You know your grant's run out
if you can only afford a pint of milk
for breakfast and a packet
of crisps for lunch – and you
eat them both for dinner.

You know your grant's run out
if your landlord is the local dogs' home.

• • •

Graduates with a first class degree
haven't understood two words:
'student' and 'bar'.

You know you are a poor student when
you have to buy one shoe at a time.

• • •

You know you're sad if
you've still got some grant money left
after the first night's revelry.

Ten things to get with your grant cheque:
1) a traffic cone 2) a sociology degree
3) what you think are drugs
4) a traffic cone 5) the NME
6) badges 7) an Oxfam coat
8) Blu tac 9) drunk 10) laid

Decorate your study so that it reflects your work habits – take out the desk and replace it with a daybed.

• • •

You know you are destined to become a chiropodist if you go to medical school but don't want to buy the whole skeleton.

You know things are getting really tough
when Oxfam sends you aid parcels.

• • •

How to spot an Oxbridge student:
they're the ones with
hand-stitched holes in their jeans.

You know your poverty is showing
when beggars try not to make eye contact.

• • •

How to get 20 students into a mini:
just let 5 out first.

Allowing a student to work behind a bar
is like giving a pyromaniac a job as a firefighter.

• • •

Try to keep to a balanced diet,
like a six-pack in each hand.

Arts students are like satellites in orbit – except
that eventually satellites come back to earth.

• • •

Confuse an arts student –
tell her to meet you in the library.

Exams are like snot –
they get up your nose.

• • •

You know political passion has died
when the most militant group you can join
is Students Against Pâté.

Only a physics student
can explain why a 2.2 = UB40.

• • •

It takes 20 students to change a lightbulb:
one to light a candle and 19 to stage a sit-in
until it gets changed for them.

27

You know your student hall is a dump when
you take a bath and it leaves a ring around you.

• • •

If you suddenly enjoy the feel of the earth
as your pillow and the sky as your roof, you must
be a student who's just failed to pay the rent.

28

The philosophy student's motto:
I think I exist, therefore I exist – I think.

• • •

Grant money is a constant worry,
but remember the Government is working
night and day to relieve you of it.

It's easy to be modest when you've got top marks.
The skill is to be arrogant when you've failed.

• • •

You know you're in trouble
if you phone your bank for a larger overdraft
and you're answered by Dial-a-Prayer.

A good tutor is one who is able to impart
knowledge without actually possessing any.

• • •

An arts degree is like a bad bra.
It leaves you well-rounded but
not pointing in any particular direction.

Don't ask how many
sociology students it takes to
change a lightbulb because it
isn't the lightbulb
that needs changing,
OK, it's society.

Social Drinking for students means drinking
to the point where no one wants to be with you.

• • •

Don't ask how many Oxbridge rowers it takes
to screw in a lightbulb because they only screw
when they're pissed.

Never put an essay off till tomorrow
that you can put off for good.

• • •

You know your student house is in a state
if it has to be done-up
before the council will condemn it.

The average student room is so small
you have to boil one egg at a time.

• • •

You know your student house
is a dump when vandals
break in and decorate it.

You know you're poor if your lunch
consists of a bean on toast.

• • •

The walls of student rooms are so thin
you can hear the people next door
changing their minds.

If you must go to lectures wear a loud shirt
to stop you falling asleep.

• • •

If you can't afford to rent a room,
disguise yourself as a banana
and sleep in the fruit bowl.

Try to stay out of debt,
even if you have to borrow money to do so.

• • •

Don't do an archaeology degree.
Your life will be in ruins.

Law students are easy –
they love looking into briefs.

• • •

Never lend money to geology students –
they think in terms of millions of years.

Remember, the real meaning of a PhD
is a Piss-head Diploma.

• • •

Also remember, the real meaning of a BA
is a Boring Arsehole.

If you get a starred first in an arts degree
you become a BA-starred.

• • •

There is one sure way of reducing graduate
unemployment – don't graduate.

There is a difference between
an increase in student grants
and Father Christmas:
there's a remote possibility that
there is a Father Christmas.

When you are a student a bank
is somewhere where you
can borrow money so long as
you can prove your parents
don't need it.

Feel a little fresher
every day.

• • •

You know you're new to college life
if you can't sniff coke because the bubbles
keep going up your nose.

Old professors never die,
they just lose their faculties.

• • •

If you are a science student you are
probably modest – but then you've got
a lot to be modest about.

E = MC Hammer.
Discuss.

• • •

The only way a science student knows
that term has ended is that
he's the only one left in the library.

What's the difference between a rag mag and the *Sun*? Rag mags cover world issues.

• • •

Student days are the best. What other time will your parents give you money to go to another town and get drunk every night?

Try not to have any original ideas –
it only leads to complications.

• • •

Student grants give you enough money
to last the whole course –
so long as you don't buy anything.

Don't even think about
mooning a werewolf.

• • •

Linguistics is a good subject to study
because when you graduate you will
truly appreciate alphabet soup.

Don't get too popular,
no one will like you.

• • •

Student grants give you enough for a roof
over your head. Of course if you want
walls and floors, that's extra.

Of course an education is important –
how else will you get your own parking space?

• • •

College law: if you finish an exam in record time
it will be because there are 13 questions
on the last page you didn't see.

51

Don't let lectures interfere
with your education.

• • •

'A penny for your thoughts'
is something you'll never hear
the Secretary for Education say.

If you're looking for true enlightenment
leave college and get a lighthouse.

• • •

Remember, at university
the key to popularity is the one
that fits the ignition.

If you want to be different
try wearing odd-coloured socks.
You'll really stand out because
most other students will be wearing
jeans and a T-shirt.

The science of casual wear – jeanetics.

• • •

You know it's time to clean out the fridge
when your leftovers start looking like
your biochemistry project.

Make sure you get a good degree so that
you can join the work farce.

• • •

Law students only have to
pass the bar once, but it doesn't stop them
going in every other time.

If your denims shrink in the wash
you'll end up with recessive jeans.

• • •

Being a student is proof that the mind
is an incredible thing –
it can be totally empty and still not cave in.

If you want to find low interest rates
pop into a lecture.

• • •

A university education helps you
to be confused about everything
at a more sophisticated level.

Definition of a highbrow:
someone who's read all the best book titles.

• • •

Some people go to college to
drink from the well of knowledge, but this
doesn't include buying their round.

Definition of a genius:
someone too clever to get a proper job.

• • •

Just when you think you know the
definition of the word 'pointless' you turn up
at a lecture that redefines it.

Tutors often have photographic minds –
underdeveloped and negative.

• • •

It's only when you graduate that you
find that life is a test and
nobody's given you the textbook.

Relative obscurity is when your overdraft
is so big your parents ignore you.

• • •

The main reason for getting a degree
is so that you can be pushed around
by a better class of person.

Whoever said money doesn't buy happiness
has never done much shopping.

• • •

Students' financial problems are
usually quite simple –
they don't have any money.

A bore is someone who got top marks
in the subject you failed.

• • •

Advice for freshers: money won't
buy you friends but it'll get you
some pretty enthusiastic aquaintances.

Life's lessons could be learnt a lot easier if
they stopped making degrees out of them.

• • •

A university education gives you confidence:
that's the ability to be wrong
with absolute conviction.

If we really profited from our mistakes,
every essay would be an earner.

• • •

Fresher law:
If the student is 2x and the lager is 4x
then the music becomes KLF.

A lecture is designed to focus your brain
on important things such as sleep.

• • •

Male undergraduates at a Freshers' Ball try to
solve the 'leg-over-blond' equation where
Hope is a constant and Max is a factor.

Any student can do
an honours at the bar.

• • •

Recipe for student spaghetti Bolognese:
chips, rice, tin of tomatoes,
no spaghetti.

An hour in a lecture can show you that things are
always dullest just before the yawn.

• • •

If you think you've got all the answers
it's probably because you
didn't understand the questions.

Exam question: Discuss student social life
with particular emphasis on the
Red Plastic Traffic Cone and why
it seems such a good idea to pinch one
at two o'clock in the morning.

Everyone knows that students
are at it like rabbits – they only eat
vegetables, they have small brains and
they spend much of their time
in dark poky burrows.

Tales of sex in the library can
usually be filed under 'Fiction'.

• • •

Student political apathy would be a problem
if anyone could be
bothered to do something about it.

72

The traffic cones hotline is really for students
wanting to decorate their rooms.

• • •

If you cross a sociology student
with the Mafia you end up
with an offer you can't understand.

73

Young Conservative students are like cream –
rich, thick and full of clots.

• • •

Money in the bank is like toothpaste in a tube –
easy to get out,
very hard to put back again.

You know you're at a tough college if the other students wear university scars.

• • •

If your tutor insists on getting inside your underwear prior to giving you a pass mark in your subject, stick a pair of knickers on his head.

Good societies to put on your CV:
   – I Love Working Society
   – Young Conservatives
– Striped Suit and Mobile Phone Fan Club
– *Financial Times* Appreciation Society.

Bad societies to put on your CV:
– Alcoholics Anonymous
– Drinking All Night and Moaning
About Your Loan Society
– Cleavage Appreciation Society
– Rubber and Bondage Support Group
– Young Marxists.

Definition of the bar –
a second home.

• • •

Definition of morning lectures –
things that are missed following nights
of heavy drinking.

Definition of student societies –
themed drinking groups.

• • •

Definition of afternoon lectures –
things that are missed following nights
of very heavy drinking.

79

Definition of work –
what you do the day before exams.

• • •

Definition of end of term holidays –
periods of sobriety during which you
try to earn some money.

80

Definition of a degree – proof that you can hold down
ten pints and still write some kind of an essay.

• • •

Summer holidays are useful times in which to
get to know your new stepparent –
and borrow money from them.

Don't think that Freshers' Balls are anything special –
they're no different to those of any other student

• • •

The only difference between a Freshers' Ball
and a meat market is that at a meat market
the sausages are bigger.

Posters not to have in your room:

A big blue one with 'Vote Conservative' on it;

A tennis player scratching her bum (how old are you?);

A chart of tyre pressures (particularly if you're an engineering student);

'Buttercups of the World' from *The Lady*.

Boaties like to have a dip in the drink –
particularly if it's beer.

• • •

Advice to freshers: don't be fooled by older
students' tales of trumped-up traditions such as
skinny-dipping in the fountain, swearing at
the principal and going to lectures.

Student luvvies can only perform if
they have an audience.

• • •

Male freshers will be disappointed to discover
that the college 'bike' is actually a two-wheeled
sit-up-and-beg with a basket at the front.

85

Useful part-time jobs for students:
– Being a cleaner in the principal's office where
the exam papers are kept
– Stacking shelves in the local off-licence
– Working as a taxi-driver where you can
wind the clock back on your car.

The word 'lecture' comes from the Latin
for 'empty room'.

• • •

The word 'student' comes from the Latin
word 'studare' which means
'to stay up late and miss lectures'.

If you think you're falling
in love with a decrepit tutor,
visit the loony bin and find out
how it affected his wife.
This should put you back on the rails.

Beware of people who
stagger up to you at the freshers' ball
and say they only went to university
to get pissed – especially
if they're your tutor.

You know your student house is damp if
Yorkshire Water visits you to fill up a tanker.

• • •

Get to know your bank manager.
Let's face it, given the size of your overdraft,
he's banking with you.

Get your hair cut!

• • •

A keen drama graduate can easily
find herself a job in the West End
uttering those immortal lines
'Would you like fries with your burger sir?'

Remember, man (and woman)
cannot live on bourbon biscuits alone.

• • •

Keep a dog. You can always say
it ate your essay. If you're really struggling
he could even write it for you.

92

The Government likes to support Britain's great universities – both of them.

• • •

The reason most students choose college rather than the University of Life is that the drinks aren't subsidised at the University of Life.

Rugger buggers like playing with pointy balls.

• • •

You don't need to give too much respect to
graduates – remember, doctors were once medical
students, lawyers were once law students and
street sweepers were once sociology students.

Footie boys like to dribble in their shorts.

• • •

A year abroad before going to university
is invaluable. It gives you a chance to expand
your horizons, build your confidence
and validate your xenophobia.

Term-time can be very stressful
so in the holidays give yourself
a complete change of lifestyle:
find out where the library is,
get some books out and write an essay.

Make an impression during
Freshers' Week by recounting your
experiences in the drug rehabilitation centre
following overdoses of tea
during your A levels.

Advice for science students:
you can make any idiotic statement
you like so long as you follow it
with the words 'This can be easily proved
by applying Einstein's equation $E = MC^2$'.

Reality bites, as you will find when you
put your card into the cashpoint machine
and the manager's face pops up saying
'You've had your £10 HMV voucher,
you sucker, now sod off'.

Recipe for student curry:
cheapo mince you bought last week that's
gone a funny green colour, a tin of curry powder,
16 tins of tomatoes. Cook in big vat from
the science block. Serve with chips.
(If you're out of mince replace
with Pedigree Chum).

Even if you have passed nothing but wind
for three years you can still
get a degree in Media Studies.

• • •

You know you're living in a complete toilet
if there are slug trails on the
kitchen floor and they read 'clean me'.

If your tutor is a letch tell him
you're not his type – you have a pulse.

• • •

Most universities enjoy student-exchange
programmes until they realise that
all they get in exchange is more students.

Think twice before you shake a veterinary
student's hand – remember where it's been.

• • •

History students should remember that
there's no such thing as new historical research –
it's all already happened, silly!

Never let a veterinary student do
the washing up with their own gloves.

• • •

Gross-out your letch of a male tutor: tell him
your battery-charged tampon remover clamps have
run out so could you borrow his sugar tongs?

Never let a veterinary student
put you down.

• • •

If you enjoy practical jokes make friends
with medical students –
they can get body parts for any occasion.

Courses parents think universities
should run to truly prepare us for life:
– Introduction to Conformity
– Nostalgia Techniques
– Principles of Disillusionment
– Conservative Behaviour
– Deceitful Job Interview Techniques
– Career Advancement Through Arse-Licking.

You know you are a true student if
your morning paper is the *Evening News*.

• • •

At college you'll meet some people who
will become your friends for life –
or until you pay back the money you owe them,
which is the same thing.

Graduate reunions can be fun unless
it's behind the counter at the local burger bar.

• • •

Your university porter will never forget you –
thirty years after you graduate he still won't
let you drive your car in.

Once they've got their degree some students
are as clever as they can be – sadly.

• • •

Tutoring in your bedsit via the Internet
now means that the only way to miss lectures is
actually to go to college.

You can judge the calibre of a university
by the size of the rock bands it attracts.
With the aim of getting Oasis rather than
Showaddywaddy, many A-level students are
picking Wembley as their first choice.

Do your bit to help the local community
by going home for the holidays
allowing the council time to replace
the missing traffic cones, road signs
and small shrubs.

Slavery still exists in this country but for political
reasons it's known as Vacation Work Experience.

• • •

Psychology students are easy to spot – they're
the ones with their knickers on their heads shouting
'I'm a potato! I'm a potato!'

Student radio – like hospital radio but
without the same consummate professionalism.

• • •

Languages students are useful to take on holiday
with you. They're usually so dull they make you
look fanciable at the local disco.

If a couple of earnest-looking students
knock on your door and ask you
if you've found God, invite them in and
give them a blow-by-blow account of
your gall-bladder operation, remembering
to show them your scars.

Don't bother with the 'milk-round'.
It is so-called because you have to
get up early to go to it, you hit lots of
dead-ends and fewer and fewer people
are interested in using your services.

Architecture students
can erect to order.

• • •

A student concession is where you let your
parents win an argument so that they'll slip
you some cash when you leave.

A student in need is
a student in deed.

• • •

Compare and contrast your chances of
getting a lucrative and fulfilling job after graduating
with the likelihood of a second coming.

You'll never get by in computer science if you keep putting tippex on the screen.

• • •

You know you're not going to make it in medicine if you spend hours in the library studying for your blood test.

A student needs a lecture like
a fish needs a bicycle.

• • •

Even before it was made a curriculum subject,
Women's Studies have been undertaken in universities
all over the country – usually in the bar.

Responses to your lecherous tutor's offers
of dinner in his study:

– I would but I just don't hate myself enough
to go through with it.

– Yeah great! I'll bring my boyfriend,
Buster the rugby captain, with me.

– I know I said I go for older men,
but not that old!

The Freshers' Ball –
what they really mean when they say…

'What A-levels did you do?'
(Are you stupid enough to come to bed with me?)

'Have you got a boyfriend here?'
(Can I bonk you insensible?)

'I've got one of the best rooms in the college.'
(I want you to spend the night in it.)

'I dunno why you chose this college –
the standards are crap.' (I'm a tutor.)

'I'm great at sex.'
(I can't wait to try it with a woman.)

Student drama – what happens when
your grant cheque is two weeks late.

• • •

Definition of a student loan – when your
clever friend lends you her notes with which
to cobble an essay together.

Acne –
the cheapest form of student contraception.

• • •

Well-known collective terms:
lions – a pride, fish – a school,
students – bloody.

Degree courses we would like to see:
Star Trek Appreciation, *Monty Python* Script
Analysis, Feces Theses.

• • •

If you ever get that feeling that everyone else is
having a great time while you're just sitting in your
room working, just remember, you're absolutely right.

Jasmine Birtles has had a long and illustrious career in academics. After winning the Cost-Cutter Scholarship in skipping lectures at Cambridge she was offered the What-She-Wants Chair of Writing Pompous Letters to *Points of View* at the University of Bolton. A leading figure in Lycra she also spent six months studying towelling behaviour amongst golfers in Wisconsin. Returning to England she held the Chair of Mathematics at the University of Tower Hamlets until it got too heavy for her and she was promoted to the Sofa of Nuclear Physics. As an animal behaviourist she has had many successes. While studying intelligence in chickens she found that under laboratory tests at Center Parcs the chickens could negotiate the maze but had trouble finding their way back on to the minibus.